# The Guilty Book

# The Guilty Book

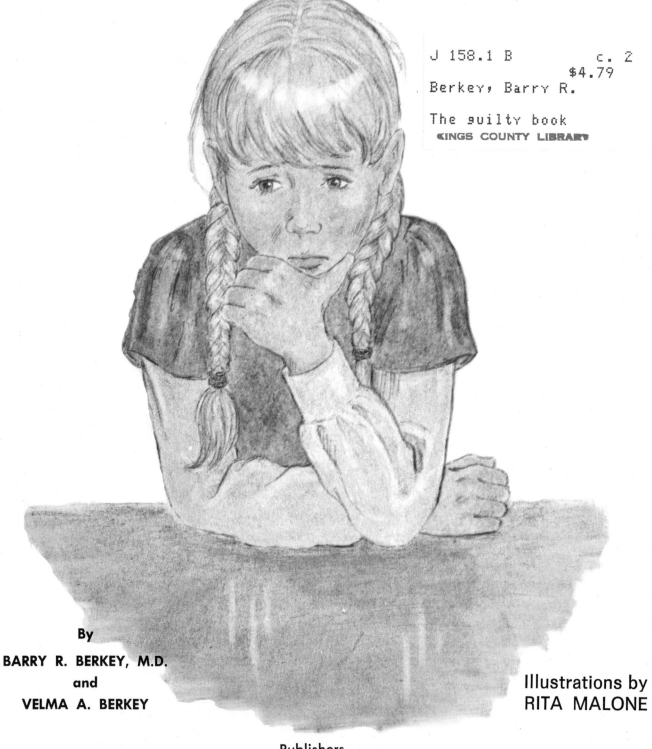

By
**BARRY R. BERKEY, M.D.**
and
**VELMA A. BERKEY**

Illustrations by
**RITA MALONE**

Publishers
T. S. DENISON & COMPANY, INC.
Minneapolis

 T. S. DENISON & COMPANY, INC.

Standard Book Number: 513-01562-0
Printed in the United States of America
Copyright © 1977 by T. S. Denison & Co., Inc.
Minneapolis, Minn. 55437

To Our Parents

REBECCA and LEONARD LEVIN

and

ESTHER and SAUL BERKEY

GUILT is a feeling that every person knows about. Both grown-ups and boys and girls know about GUILT.

GUILT is not a nice feeling, but everybody feels GUILTY now and then. It is a normal way to feel once in a while.

Grown-ups, like parents and teachers, sometimes speak about a GUILTY CONSCIENCE. This is just a different way of talking about GUILTY feelings.

GUILTY FEELINGS COME WHEN SOMEONE DOES A BAD THING THAT HE IS SORRY ABOUT.

There is a boy whose name is Billy. He is nine years old and he has a sister named Susan. She is six.

One day Billy broke Susan's talking doll, and he didn't tell her. When she saw it was broken, she said, "Who broke my doll?" She cried and cried, because it was a special birthday present. Billy knew it was her favorite toy, and when he saw Susan cry, he felt very bad. He was sorry he broke her doll, and he was even more sorry he didn't tell her right away.

The feeling Billy had was GUILT.

SOMETIMES GUILTY FEELINGS COME WHEN YOU DO **NOT** DO SOMETHING YOU SHOULD DO.

Billy had three big beautiful box turtles which lived in a wire turtle pen in his back yard. Susan and Billy and many of their friends had fun playing with the pet turtles. They had turtle races, and they tried to guess which turtle would win.

Billy took care of the turtles. It was Billy's job to feed the turtles and clean the pen, but during the summer he forgot to feed them for three whole weeks. They became weak and sick. A few days later the turtles died.

Billy felt terrible. He was very sad.

Susan said, "Don't worry, Billy, you didn't do it on purpose. You just forgot."

But Billy still felt very sorry. He felt GUILTY because he did not do something he should have done.

WHERE DO GUILTY FEELINGS COME FROM?

They

come

from

the

MIND.

# HOW DO GUILTY FEELINGS GET INSIDE THE MIND?

When you were younger, your parents taught you not to lie or steal or cheat in games. They told you not to hit your baby brother or sister. They explained what was a nice way to behave and what was not nice.

Parents sometimes punish children for doing bad things.

Parents, aunts, uncles, grandparents, teachers, police-men, and lots of other grown-ups explain rules to follow and live by. They explain what is nice and what is not, what is right and what is wrong. You learn from grown-ups.

You learn to be nice.

You learn to follow rules.

PLEASE
DO NOT PICK
THE FLOWERS

As you grow older, parents and teachers do not need to explain as much about behavior. As you grow older, you learn from your parents and from other grown-ups whom you like and admire. You become used to their rules.

PLEASE
DO NOT PICK
THE FLOWERS

The rules of parents and teachers slowly become your own rules to live by.

This is how children get a CONSCIENCE.

Children usually add some rules of their own to the rules learned from grown-ups.

Once you learn the rules of right and wrong, they become part of you because you know them so well. When you do NOT follow the rules and do wrong things, GUILT feelings come.

After a while children usually forget that their own ideas of right and wrong were once the ideas of parents and teachers. Good behavior becomes a habit. The rules you live by seem to have always been inside you.

You may even behave like your parents toward a younger brother or sister. You may teach a younger sister what is nice and not nice.

After you have your own CONSCIENCE, it takes the place of parents, teachers, policemen and other grown-ups. You no longer need anyone else to tell you if you are good or bad. Your own CONSCIENCE tells you whether you are good or bad. Feelings of GUILT come from the CONSCIENCE in your MIND.

If you do something you know is wrong, after you have your CONSCIENCE, you feel GUILTY. Even if no one sees you doing something wrong, you still know it is wrong, and you feel GUILTY.

Robbie is ten years old. She went across the street to play with her friend Linda. When Robbie was at Linda's house, Robbie took a special stamp from Linda's stamp book. No one saw Robbie sneak the stamp into her purse.

That night when Robbie was undressed and ready for bed, she thought, "I stole Linda's best stamp. I wouldn't like it if I had invited her to my house and she stole one of my stamps."

Robbie thought and thought. The next day she took the stamp back to Linda because she felt GUILTY.

Robbie felt proud because she took it back when no one told her to. Her GUILTY CONSCIENCE went away. She never stole again.

Robbie has a healthy CONSCIENCE. Her GUILT feelings helped her to be a nice person.

WHEN SOMEBODY FEELS GUILTY ALMOST ALL THE TIME, SOMETHING IS WRONG.

Some girls and boys feel GUILTY almost all the time. This happens when too many rules from too many people become part of you. Then your GUILTY CONSCIENCE grows too strong. You feel GUILTY for things you should not feel GUILTY about. It is a terrible way to feel.

A boy named Jack has a super-strong GUILTY CON-SCIENCE.

Jack carried out the trash for his mother every day. He hated carrying trash, but he would never disobey his mother.

One day a neighbor boy named Don saw Jack. Don was sitting in his wheelchair. He could not walk. When Don was little, he had a bad sickness that made his legs too weak to walk.

Don started to cry when he saw Jack dumping the trash in the garbage can.

"What's wrong, Don?" asked Jack.

"I wish I could walk like you," said Don. "I wish I could carry out the trash."

Jack did not know what to say to Don, so he went inside his house. He started to cry. He felt GUILTY because he hated carrying the trash. "Poor Don would be glad to carry out the trash. He'd be glad to do anything if only he could walk," Jack said to himself.

"Im a bad person," Jack thought. He cried even more.
He felt GUILTY.

Something is wrong inside Jack. His GUILTY CON-
SCIENCE is too strong. He feels GUILTY almost all the
time. This time it was because of the trash and what
Don said.

Jack didn't do anything wrong. It wasn't his fault that
Don could not walk. Jack's feelings became all mixed
up. He began to feel very sad and GUILTY almost all
the time.

WHEN SOMEONE NEVER FEELS GUILTY, SOMETHING IS ALSO WRONG.

This happens when rules from parents, teachers, and other grown-ups do not become part of your own rules to live by. When a boy or girl does not learn what is right and wrong, they do not get a CONSCIENCE, or if they do, they get a tiny, weak CONSCIENCE.

Sally lives on the same street as Don and Jack. She is very different from Jack.

One day when Sally was coming home from school, she saw Don trying to play basketball from his wheelchair. Don tried and tried to make a basket, but he could not even toss the ball as high as the hoop.

 'You're really dumb, Don," Sally said. "You can't play basketball. Don't you know that? You can't even walk. I'll bet you can't even stand up."

Sally was very mean, and she didn't care.

Sally was very mean, and she didn't care if she hurt Don's feelings.

Don began to cry. He felt sad, and started to wheel his chair to his front door.

Sally didn't care about how sad she made Don feel. She had no feelings of GUILT. She didn't have any friends. No one liked her because she was mean to a lot of others besides Don.

Sally had a very weak CONSCIENCE.

Sally's feelings were mixed up. Jack's feelings were mixed up. Both Sally and Jack had something wrong with their CONSCIENCES.

The problem that Sally has with her CONSCIENCE is a different kind of problem than Jack has with his CON-SCIENCE.

What is wrong with Sally's CONSCIENCE? Is it too strong or too weak?

What is wrong with Jack's CONSCIENCE?

Jack's and Sally's mixed-up feelings mean they need to make their mixed-up feelings HEALTHY again. Jack and Sally are not happy the way they are.

Somebody must help them. Maybe Jack's and Sally's parents can help them. Maybe an aunt or uncle can help.

There are times when boys and girls — like Jack and Sally — need to see a special kind of doctor. When their feelings get really mixed up, a doctor who knows a lot about the MIND and about feelings may have to help them get a HEALTHY CONSCIENCE.

The doctor who knows about feelings, like GUILTY feelings, is a PSYCHIATRIST. He can help.

The PSYCHIATRIST helps by talking about mixed-up feelings.

A doctor can help Jack not feel GUILTY all the time. He can help Jack understand that his CONSCIENCE is too strong. Slowly Jack can learn that he is not a bad person. He can learn to have fun and be happy. As his CONSCIENCE gets weaker, Jack will not feel GUILTY most of the time. Then he will be happy.

A PSYCHIATRIST can also help Sally to make her CON-SCIENCE stronger. Slowly, as Sally learns what is right and what is nice behavior, her GUILTY CONSCIENCE will grow stronger. When this happens, Sally will become a nicer person. She will learn to understand the feeling of others, and she will then make friends because she will not be cruel to them. Sally will become a nicer person and she will feel happy, too.

# ACKNOWLEDGEMENTS

We would like to thank the following individuals for their help. Joan Boysen; Mildred Dobson; Albert L. Fortune, Principal, Commonwealth Christian School, Fairfax, Virginia; Anne Garrett; Joyce Goodman, Principal, Congressional Schools, Falls Church, Virginia; Kathleen Hauser; Flora Jackson; Joanne Lonergan; Thomas B. Lyles, Principal, Wakefield Forest Elementary School, Fairfax, Virginia; Obed Malone, Headmaster, East End Primary, Tortola, British West Indies; Peter M. Manno, Principal, Oak View Elementary School, Fairfax, Virginia; Irma Moke; Margaret Newhall; Winston A. Rhymer, Principal, St. Mary's School, Virgin Gorda, British Virgin Islands; and Patricia Smith.

The teachers assisted us by giving their time and effort, and by having their students prepare over 1000 papers on "feelings." The principals' cooperation and active participation through their staff added an essential dimension for which we are grateful.

## ABOUT THE AUTHORS

Barry Robert Berkey, a physician-author who specializes in psychiatry, emphasizes marital and family therapy. His most recent book is SAVE YOUR MARRIAGE (Nelson-Hall Publishing Co.) Dr. Berkey is a diplomate of the American Board of Psychiatry and Neurology, and a Fellow of the American Psychiatric Association.

Velma Berkey is a graduate of the University of Pittsburgh, School of Education. Before becoming a professional writer, she taught elementary education in the public schools. She and Dr. Berkey, as a husband-wife team, emphasize emotions in most of their children's books. They have authored several other works including THE MIND IS A FUNNY THING (T. S. Denison) and CHINCOTEAGUE FOR CHILDREN with their son, Richard Berkey, (Tidewater Publishers).

Rita Malone, a noted artist who specializes in children's artwork, has illustrated three books by Dr. and Mrs. Berkey.